DEMOLITION RICHES

The Investor's Guide to Profiting from Tear-Downs, Fire-Damaged Homes, and Court-Released Properties

By: Sienna Reed

Contents

Chapter 1: Understanding the Demolition Market

Demolition properties represent one of the most overlooked—and misunderstood—opportunities in real estate investing. These buildings are often the worst on the block: structurally unsound, severely damaged, code-violating, fire-scarred, or environmental hazards. To the untrained eye, they look like liabilities. But to the strategic investor, they are **hidden assets**, access points to high-upside development, infill construction, and discounted urban lots that most people ignore or fear.

What makes these properties so powerful is **how off-market they are**. While everyone else is chasing flips on the MLS or battling for turnkey rentals on Zillow, demolition properties live quietly in **city databases, housing court records, code enforcement logs, and land bank inventories**. They are **not advertised**, and they don't attract competition—unless you know exactly where to look.

The key to unlocking this opportunity lies in understanding how cities enforce property safety, assign legal risk, and determine demolition orders. Every municipality has its own process, but most operate on the same fundamentals: They identify public nuisance properties, conduct inspections, assign violation notices, and eventually submit orders for demolition when the structure is deemed irreparable or dangerous.

These properties are often in legal limbo—**stuck between ownership disputes, unpaid taxes, open environmental concerns, and bureaucratic red tape**—a reason why traditional investors avoid them. But if you can learn to navigate this process using city records, attending court hearings, or contacting the owners of at-risk buildings, you can **acquire properties for pennies on the dollar** before they ever hit public auction.

Beyond the pricing, the location is key. Demolition-designated properties are often found in transitioning neighborhoods. These are usually **urban cores undergoing revitalization, infill development, or zoning upgrades**. In these zones, the land value alone may outweigh the structure, and once the building is demolished, you hold a buildable lot with city utilities, street access, and a legal address already in place.

Moreover, these deals offer **flexibility** in your exit strategy. You can:

- Flip the land to a developer
- Partner with a modular or tiny home builder
- Sell to nonprofit housing groups
- Build new construction tailored to local demand
- Hold as vacant land with minimal carrying costs until value appreciates

The entry point is low, sometimes within a range as little as **$1 to $20,000.** However, the potential upside can be ten to twenty times, if executed properly.

Of course, it's not without risk. Demolition properties come with **structural liabilities, legal barriers, environmental unknowns, and fast-moving timelines**. Cities don't wait. Once demolition orders are signed and funding is approved, the bulldozers move quickly. You must be ready to act, fund, and coordinate demo work fast—or risk losing the opportunity.

But for investors who do their homework—build relationships with city departments and understand how to navigate off-market acquisition—**the demolition market offers a rare blend of low cost and high control**.

This chapter will break down how demolition properties are defined, categorized, and sourced, and how to position yourself as a buyer when everyone else sees a teardown.

By the end of it, where others see destruction, you'll learn to spot **a rebuild-ready canvas**.

Let's begin.

What Is a Demolition Property?

A **demolition property** is any building that a city, housing court, or municipal code enforcement office has legally designated for teardown due to unsafe conditions. These properties are considered a danger to public health, structural integrity, or neighborhood stability. Demolition orders are typically issued when rehabilitation is no longer cost-effective or when the risk of collapse or contamination is deemed too high.

Unlike traditional properties, demolition properties are not found on the

MLS. They live in **off-market systems**: court dockets, city inspector reports, code enforcement lists, or public notices. Finding these properties requires direct access to municipal databases or attendance at local housing or demolition hearings.

The four most common reasons a property is ordered for demolition include:

1. Structural Collapse Risk

A property may be flagged for demolition if it poses a risk of **physical collapse**. This includes buildings with compromised foundations, leaning exterior walls, buckled roofs, sagging joists, or extensive water damage that has weakened structural supports. Often, these properties have been abandoned for years and deteriorated due to neglect, vandalism, or severe weather. In such cases, municipal inspectors conduct structural assessments and may declare the building "dangerous" or "beyond feasible repair."

For investors, these properties present a major opportunity when located in redevelopment zones. Once demolished, the land underneath becomes buildable and typically retains utility hookups, zoning entitlements, and street access.

2. Extensive Fire Damage

Properties that have been impacted by **major fires** often become candidates for demolition. Fire-damaged homes are structurally unstable, pose a risk of collapse, and may carry dangerous soot, smoke residue, and carbon contamination. While some fire-damaged properties can be salvaged, those with significant damage to roof structures, load-bearing walls, or electrical systems are often declared uninhabitable. Insurance claims may still be pending, which can delay sales or title transfers. However, once cleared, the lots can become **prime redevelopment opportunities**. Investors with expertise in rebuilding or working with modular homes can capitalize on these underpriced assets with minimal competition.

3. Environmental Hazard

Environmental risks—**asbestos, mold infestation, underground oil tanks, or lead contamination**—can cause a property to be declared unsafe and flagged for demolition. Properties built before 1978 have a higher chance of containing hazardous materials, including lead paint and outdated plumbing systems. Cities may mandate demolition when the cost of remediation exceeds a certain threshold or when cleanup is deemed infeasible within residential safety standards. For investors, it's critical to conduct environmental assessments before acquiring such properties. While environmental hazards increase upfront costs, once cleared, the lots can often qualify for local remediation grants or redevelopment tax credits.

4. **Legal Non-Compliance or Nuisance Declaration**

If a property is subject to ongoing **code violations**, harbors illegal activity, becomes a hub for squatters, or is abandoned to the point of attracting criminal behavior or pests, a municipality may declare it a **public nuisance**. These designations are often assigned in housing court, not on listing services. In many cases, owners are absentee, deceased, or unwilling to pay fines or restore the property. After multiple citations, the court may issue a demolition order to ensure neighborhood safety and stability. These properties are often excellent candidates for acquisition if you can **contact the heir, negotiate lien releases, or partner with the city on revitalization.**

Where to Find Them

These properties are rarely marketed by agents. You won't find them on Zillow, Redfin, or your local MLS. Instead, you need to **dig into the data**, pull public code violation lists, scour demolition orders filed by the housing department, attend court proceedings, and review municipal notices posted in city clerks' offices or online databases.

Demolition properties are public—but invisible to most.

If you learn where to look, you gain access to a market few investors touch. A market where **opportunity lives beneath the rubble.**

City-Ordered Demolitions

These are properties formally targeted by the city for demolition due to severe code violations, structural instability, or classification as a public nuisance. In many cases, these buildings have remained vacant for years, accumulating complaints, citations, and safety concerns. Once the city deems the property a threat to health or neighborhood integrity, it issues a demolition order.

These properties are often listed on public nuisance or blight removal databases and may carry attached liens for code enforcement fines or cleanup costs. However, if the demolition has not yet been executed, investors can often intervene and **acquire the property at deeply discounted rates**, sometimes through direct negotiation with the owner or city.

By assuming responsibility for demolition, cleanup, and redevelopment, you may also gain access to **city incentives, grants, or land write-down programs** designed to encourage revitalization in struggling neighborhoods.

Fire-Damaged Homes

These properties have experienced moderate to severe fire damage, often resulting in structural instability, smoke contamination, or significant interior loss. While some are total losses, others can be **partially salvaged**, especially if the foundation and framing are intact.

Fire-damaged homes are typically flagged by local inspectors and may sit in limbo during **insurance investigations or claims processing**. For investors, the key is to understand/evaluate the extent of damage, the cost of cleanup, and whether the property can be restored. These homes are frequently off-market and may be sold by overwhelmed owners, heirs, or insurance companies looking to avoid further liability. If purchased strategically, they offer significant upside.

Investors with strong construction teams or modular home partners can clear the site and **rebuild faster than traditional development timelines**, taking advantage of reduced competition and discounted entry points.

Condemned Properties

Condemned homes have been officially declared **unfit for human occupancy** by local authorities. These designations are issued due to serious structural, electrical, plumbing, or environmental hazards.

A condemned property may have partial roof collapse, exposed wiring, sewage backup, black mold, or be completely boarded up and inaccessible. They are often **red-tagged** and posted with warning notices, and may have been vacated by tenants or owners under court order.

Most of these homes require full rehab or demolition and come with layers of legal and permitting complexity. However, these properties are often in **densely populated urban areas** with high land value. For the right investor—especially those with experience navigating municipal processes—they offer the opportunity to **secure prime lots for redevelopment**, often at less than tax-assessed value.

Acquiring and clearing a condemned property can also improve neighborhood safety and boost long-term appreciation potential.

Vacant Property Acquisitions

These properties are technically not yet demo-ordered, but are at high risk due to abandonment. Many are held by heirs in probate, lost in title disputes, or left to decay due to back taxes or legal uncertainty.

Vacant homes attract vandalism, break-ins, and become safety hazards, which can eventually lead to demolition proceedings if left unaddressed. However, because they aren't yet flagged as nuisance properties, they present a unique window for **preemptive acquisition**.

Investors can locate these homes through USPS vacancy data, utility shutoff records, tax lien lists, or visual drive-by inspections. Contacting heirs, buying out tax certificates, or quieting title through legal action are common acquisition paths. These deals require more **front-end legal work**, but they can be secured far below market value and converted into full-scale rehabs, teardowns, or infill builds with the right team and strategy.

Land Bank Holdings

Land banks are municipal or county-controlled entities that hold title to vacant, abandoned, or tax-delinquent properties. These properties are typically acquired through foreclosure, donation, or code enforcement seizure and are often demo-cleared.

These properties exist to return blighted parcels back to productive use and may offer properties for as little as **$1–$5,000**, especially to local investors, builders, or nonprofits. Many land banks partner with housing authorities, modular builders, or community development organizations and may offer **site plans, grant opportunities, or zoning waivers** to speed up redevelopment. Each land bank has its own rules, eligibility criteria, and application process. These holdings are especially valuable in **opportunity zones, revitalization districts, or areas with planned infrastructure investment.**

For investors who are patient, civic-minded, and willing to engage with public-sector bureaucracy, land banks represent one of the most **affordable paths to urban land acquisition** in the country.

Let me know when you're ready for the next section: **Key Benefits for Investors**, or if you'd like this turned into a downloadable demo deal sourcing matrix!

Acquire for $1 to $20K in Some Cities

One of the most attractive aspects of demolition property investing is the **ultra-low acquisition cost**. In cities with aggressive blight reduction programs, such as Detroit, Cleveland, St. Louis, Chicago, and Buffalo, municipalities are offloading distressed properties for as little as **$1 to $20,000**.

These properties may be slated for teardown or already demo-cleared and sold as vacant land. As they often carry legal or environmental baggage, traditional buyers avoid them, creating an opportunity for the investor who knows how to navigate public records, code violations, and land bank programs. These steep discounts give you a unique margin buffer, allowing for significant ROI even with substantial demo or rebuild costs. The low entry point also means **less capital at risk**, making these projects ideal for cash buyers, private lenders, or investor partnerships looking to scale without massive upfront investment.

Access to Infill Lots in Hot Urban Zones

As cities grow and urban cores undergo revitalization, infill development becomes a central focus for planners and developers. Demolition properties are often located in **prime infill zones**: neighborhoods close to downtown, near transit hubs, schools, or commercial corridors. As teardown homes are frequently in older housing stock neighborhoods, they tend to sit on **existing infrastructure**—utilities, sidewalks, sewer— making them ideal for new development. Unlike greenfield development, which may require major upfront investment in roads and services, infill lots are often **ready to build** once cleared.

These lots also carry historical address registration, which simplifies permitting and zoning review. For investors who understand local development trends, demo deals can offer access to **high-appreciation zones** where buildable land is scarce. When others are bidding on rehabs, you're controlling land in the path of progress, that too at a fraction of the price.

Potential to Develop Custom New Construction or Modular Infill Housing

Once a demo property is cleared, it becomes a **blank canvas**, allowing you to design and develop housing that matches current market demand. Whether you're building custom single-family homes, duplexes, modular infill units, or even tiny home clusters, the lot offers flexibility not found in traditional rehab scenarios.

As many demo properties are located in cities pushing for affordable housing, infill grants or modular home incentives may be available to reduce construction costs. Partnering with a modular builder can also significantly shorten construction timelines, turning a 6-8-month project into a 60-90-day build cycle.

New construction also allows you to maximize value with **contemporary layouts, energy-efficient materials, and better resale pricing**. Instead of being constrained by outdated plumbing, asbestos walls, or cracked foundations, you start fresh. You have a chance to build with smarter, faster, and with far fewer surprises.

Low Holding Costs Post-Demo If Land-Banked

After a property has been demolished and properly cleared, your monthly carrying costs are **dramatically reduced**. With no structure on-site, you're no longer liable for code enforcement tickets related to blight, occupancy violations, or structural instability.

Property taxes on vacant land are typically far lower than improved properties. Additionally, insurance requirements are minimal or optional. If the property is held through a city land bank or under a public-private partnership, you may also be granted **holding extensions**, tax abatements, or even funding assistance as long as your long-term plan aligns with the city's redevelopment goals. This means you can hold land in appreciating neighborhoods **without pressure to immediately build**, giving you time to secure financing, finalize designs, or align with strategic partners.

Smart demo investors use this window to plan deliberately, negotiate from a place of control, and **sell or develop at peak timing** rather than being forced into premature exits.

Legal Complexity (Court Releases, Code Violations)

One of the most significant challenges in purchasing demolition properties is navigating the **legal web** surrounding title, liens, code enforcement, and demolition orders. These properties are often tied up in **housing court proceedings**, probate disputes, or foreclosure actions. Before you can even acquire the clear title, you may need to negotiate with multiple parties, including heirs, city attorneys, or lienholders. Additionally, many properties carry **years of unpaid code violations** or fines that need to be cleared before transfer. Failure to identify these issues early can lead to stalled closings or surprise costs post-acquisition. Investors must perform **deep due diligence**: pulling violation histories, requesting municipal lien searches, and confirming that the title is insurable. Working with a title attorney experienced in distressed property law is crucial. If not handled properly, the legal issues surrounding demo properties can quickly eat into your profit margins or derail your entire exit strategy.

Environmental Remediation (Asbestos, Lead)

Older demolition properties, especially those built before 1980, commonly contain **environmental hazards** such as asbestos insulation, lead-based paint, underground oil tanks, or even illegal dumping. Before a demo permit can be issued, most cities require a **pre-demolition environmental inspection** to ensure these hazards are identified and removed properly.

Remediation is highly regulated and must be completed by **licensed professionals**, which significantly increases costs. Asbestos removal alone can range from $3,000 to $20,000, depending on the size and condition of the structure. Failure to follow proper protocols can result in **legal penalties, fines, or demolition delays**. Investors must budget for this from the beginning and should obtain written quotes from certified remediation companies during due diligence. Some cities offer grants or tax incentives for brownfield cleanup or environmental rehabilitation, but the upfront cash requirements and time delays make this a key risk area in demo deal investing.

Short Time Windows Before the City Demolishes

When a city issues a demolition order, there is usually a **limited time window** before the bulldozers arrive. Once the city allocates funding, it schedules contractors and proceeds with demolition, sometimes **within 30 to 90 days** of the order being finalized.

If you're hoping to acquire the property before the demo occurs, you must act fast. This means lining up funding, securing title, and negotiating with owners or city officials at lightning speed. In many cases, the property owner may not even be aware of the demo status, or they may be unresponsive, creating further delays. If you can't intervene in time, the building will be demolished, and any investment opportunity will be lost. Worse, if you acquire the property without knowing the city has already scheduled demolition, you could **inherit demo costs** or lose a structure you intended to salvage.

Speed, awareness, and real-time communication with city inspectors are critical.

Lack of Lending — Must Be Cash or Hard Money Driven

Traditional lenders typically **won't touch** demolition properties. As these buildings are deemed uninhabitable or structurally unsound, they don't qualify for conventional mortgage underwriting or appraisal standards. Most banks won't issue loans for properties flagged for teardown or carrying active code violations. This means you'll need **cash, private money, or hard money** to acquire, demo, and potentially redevelop the property.

Hard money lenders may be open to funding the project based on the **after-repair value (ARV)** or the land's future development potential, but interest rates are higher and terms are shorter, adding pressure to execute quickly.

Without financing, your pool of competitors may shrink, but your **capital requirements rise substantially**. Investors must build relationships with alternative lenders or maintain sufficient liquidity to fund both acquisition and cleanup. Being undercapitalized is one of the biggest reasons new investors fail to succeed in the demo property market.

Real-Life Case Study:

"From Fire Lot to $215K Sale" — Chicago, IL

An investor acquired a fire-damaged property for $7,000 from the city demolition list.

Cleared asbestos for $5,000.

Demolished for $12,000.

Partnered with a modular builder for a 3-bed home on the lot.

Sold to a first-time buyer for $215,000.

Timeline: 9 months.

Net profit: ~$91,000.

Template:

Demo Property Evaluation Checklist

☑	Criteria	Notes
☐	Address & parcel info pulled from city records	
☐	Verified demolition status (open/closed case)	
☐	Ownership confirmed	
☐	Presence of city liens	
☐	Title condition (clouded /clean)	
☐	Access to lot for inspection	
☐	Estimated demo cost ($8K–$25K typical)	
☐	Zoning/buildable lot status	
☐	Resale or redevelopment strategy	

Investor Fast Track Recap

- Demo deals live *off-market*—tap into public records, not realtors.
- Always research legal status, liens, and environmental risk before committing.
- Look for **fire-damaged**, **condemned**, or **city-owned lots**.
- Use a checklist, like the one above, to streamline your initial analysis.

Chapter 2: Sourcing Strategies That Work

Quick Start Summary

Most real estate investors fail before they begin because they simply don't know where to look.

Demolition properties don't advertise themselves. They're buried in government records, probate courts, fire department logs, and city demo dockets. This chapter teaches you how to systematically locate properties *before* they're demolished, *before* they're auctioned, and *before* your competitors ever hear about them. Mastering these sourcing strategies puts you in control of an overlooked, underpriced, and highly profitable market.

Rethinking Real Estate Leads

The path to demolition riches starts with one shift in mindset:
These deals are not found—they are uncovered.

You won't see them on Zillow. They rarely show up on the MLS. Realtors often ignore them. But cities, counties, fire marshals, and courts are overloaded with these problematic properties, and they're quietly begging someone to take them off their hands.

Unlike retail flips, where you buy a distressed property in plain sight, **demolition investing is a game of discovery**. You're hunting through hidden records, tracing abandoned titles, identifying condemned structures, and making contact before the city bulldozer arrives.

The Five Golden Sources of Demo Deals

1. City Demolition Lists (Demo Dockets)

Nearly every U.S. city maintains a running list of structures slated for demolition. These include fire-damaged properties, abandoned homes, or buildings with code violations beyond repair. These lists are public records but rarely get published widely. Some cities post them online; others require in-person requests.

Investor Play: Request the demo list from your local building department, housing court, or code enforcement office. Sort by zip code and cross-reference with recent development trends.

2. Fire Department Incident Reports

Fire-damaged homes are high-value targets. The fire department logs every call, often with addresses, levels of damage, and reports. Many owners walk away post-insurance claim, leaving properties primed for demolition—and investors.

Investor Play: File a Freedom of Information Act (FOIA) request to access fire damage logs by address and date range. Prioritize multi-unit or corner-lot properties in gentrifying areas.

3. Code Violation Logs

Homes with repeated code enforcement issues—rodents, structural rot, roof collapse, unsecured entry—eventually get flagged for demo. Cities often publish these logs weekly or monthly.

Investor Play: Subscribe to your city's open data portal or enforcement bulletin. Focus on properties with 3+ violations or active nuisance abatement status.

4. Probate & Inherited Property Records

When a property owner dies without an estate plan, the property often sits vacant. Many heirs live out of state, want nothing to do with the burden, and will happily sign it over if you solve the legal issue.

Investor Play: Search your county's probate filings weekly. Identify estates with real property assets but no probate activity. Use obituary searches and skip tracing to contact heirs directly.

5. Land Bank & Tax Delinquent Listings

Cities and counties often hold huge inventories of foreclosed, forfeited, or tax-delinquent properties. Many are demo candidates with active or completed teardowns. These can often be acquired within a range as low as $1–$5,000.

Investor Play: Contact your county land bank. Ask for the "buildable inventory" list and the requirements for development purchase. Some cities even offer demolition reimbursement programs to speed up revitalization.

Tools and Tactics for Smarter Sourcing

Use GIS Mapping Tools

Geographic Information System (GIS) maps show property parcels, ownership history, zoning, and even building footprints. Overlay demo lists or code violations to visualize opportunity zones.

- Recommended Tools: Regrid, LandGrid, Local Assessor Maps

Court Record Scraping

Use tools like PublicData or state-specific databases to search for nuisance lawsuits, foreclosure cases, and demolition orders tied to properties.

Automation and Alerts

Set up Google Alerts, county RSS feeds, or scraping bots to alert you to new code violations, probate filings, or fire incidents in target zip codes.

Contacting the Right People Early

Who You Should Be Talking To:

- Code Enforcement Officers
- Land Bank Directors
- Housing Court Clerks
- Probate Court Coordinators
- Local Fire Marshals
- Neighborhood stabilization officers

These people know what's coming before it hits any public list.

Investor Script (To a City Official):

"Hi, my name is Calyn. I'm working on a local initiative to reclaim and redevelop unsafe structures in [City]. I'd like to request the current demolition docket and understand how to participate in the city's reuse or redevelopment program. I'm prepared to meet your compliance timeline."

Case Example: The Demo List Goldmine

Location: Kansas City, MO
Process: The Investor obtained the city demolition list via FOIA. Located 4 homes within 3 blocks of a major development project. Contacted code officer, paused demolition, bought 3 of 4 homes from absentee owners for

under $10K each. Paid $14K for demo and backfill. Sold each lot with rendering and site plan for $45K+ to local builder network.

Total Net Gain: $98,000 on three lots in under 90 days.

Build a Demo Deal Pipeline

Use this weekly rhythm:

Day	Action
Monday	Check local code violations/demo orders
Tuesday	File any FOIA requests or court scrubs
Wednesday	Run skip traces on 5 new targets
Thursday	Contact owners, heirs, or legal reps
Friday	Submit demo stay requests/builder plans
Weekend	Drive past the top 3 target properties and photograph

Consistency is the difference between an opportunist and a professional.

Embedded Toolkit: Demo Sourcing Master File

You'll use a centralized file (spreadsheet or CRM) to manage:

- Property address + parcel ID
- Current legal status
- Ownership or estate status
- Estimated demo costs
- Zoning/buildability
- Contact log
- Strategy tag (Flip Lot / Modular Build / Hold & Rent)

Investor Fast Track Recap

- Demolition properties won't come to you—you have to dig.

- The best sourcing methods: **demo lists, fire reports, code violations, probate cases, and land banks.**
- Automate your process with GIS tools, alerts, and weekly research rituals.
- Contact city and county personnel early. Respect the process, build rapport, and act professionally.
- Maintain a pipeline of 10–20 active leads, track religiously, and make 3–5 contacts per week.

Chapter 3: Legal & Ownership Research: Uncovering the Truth Before You Invest

Quick Start Summary

Before swinging a sledgehammer or wiring funds, demolition property investors must **verify legal standing**. A condemned or fire-damaged property may look cheap on the surface, but if it's tangled in liens, heir disputes, or active court orders, it could become a financial black hole. This chapter teaches you how to perform legal reconnaissance: how to investigate title, trace heirs, negotiate with municipalities, and legally unlock properties that others have written off. Success in this space is not about finding deals; it's about clearing paths.

What You Don't Know Can Bankrupt You

In traditional real estate, title companies, realtors, and lenders do most of the behind-the-scenes vetting. In demolition investing, **you are the underwriter**. You're acquiring "problem properties." This means you must anticipate the red tape: quiet title actions, demolition liens, code enforcement fines, inherited property with multiple heirs, and properties stuck in legal limbo.

This is not a reason to panic. It's a reason to prepare.

Remember, **money is in the problems you can solve**, not in the ones you can avoid.

Confirming Ownership and Title Status

Step 1: Run a Title Search

A title search tells you who legally owns the property and what claims exist against it. If you're operating at scale, develop a relationship with a local title company or use services like:

- PropStream
- DataTree
- Local County Recorder's Office

Key Fields to Look For:

- Owner of Record
- Chain of Title (past 3–5 years)
- Open Liens
- Mortgages or Judgments
- Active Tax Sale or Foreclosure

If the title reads "Estate of [Name]" or shows a deceased owner, proceed to probate research immediately.

Step 2: Determine Title Condition

Condition	Risk Level	Action
Clean Title	Low	Proceed to contract
Title in deceased person's name	Medium	Locate heirs / Quiet Title Action
Multiple owners / LLC transfer	Medium	Verify signer authority
Active tax foreclosure	High	Wait or purchase post-auction
Demo lien recorded	Medium–High	Request payoff from the city

The Power of Probate & Heir Tracing

One of the most profitable—and misunderstood—aspects of demolition investing is **heir property**.

Many condemned homes are owned by someone who died 5-15 years ago. No will. No probate. Unpaid taxes. The city has no one to serve notice to, so it just marks the property for demolition.

But if you can locate the heirs… you can unlock the deed.

Steps to Trace Heirs:

6. Search public death records or obituaries
7. Cross-reference next of kin using BeenVerified or PeopleFinder
8. Look for the last known address and surviving relatives
9. Confirm identity via social media, Ancestry.com, or public filings
10. Reach out respectfully with an offer to purchase and cover legal fees

Tip: Use an Affidavit of Heirship + Quitclaim Deeds signed by all heirs. Then file a Quiet Title to clear ownership.

Understanding Demolition Liens

If the city has already demolished the property—or scheduled it—you'll likely face a **demolition lien**. These are placed to recover the cost of tearing down the structure and often range from $8,000 to more than $25,000.

But here's the secret: **They are negotiable**.

How to Handle Demo Liens?

- Request a payoff letter from the Treasurer or Code Enforcement Office
- Offer 30-50% of the balance if you submit a redevelopment plan
- Pay in cash and request lien release in writing
- Record lien satisfaction with the county clerk

Navigating Nuisance and Court Filings

Some properties have **active nuisance cases** tied to them in housing court. These are legal complaints filed by the city for violations such as:

- Unsafe structure
- Squatter activity
- Environmental hazards
- Fire hazards

How to Intervene:

- Visit housing court clerk and request the case file
- File a motion to intervene (if under contract to buy)
- Submit a redevelopment or demolition plan with your petition
- Request a stay on any active demolition order

Pro tip: Cities prefer a responsible new owner who will rehab legally over paying to demolish and maintain a vacant lot.

Checklist: Legal Recon Before You Commit

- ☑ Pull current deed & owner of record
- ☑ Search for open liens (demo, utility, taxes, judgments)
- ☑ Check demolition list and status
- ☑ Search the housing court for active enforcement
- ☑ Verify zoning for rebuild or resale
- ☑ Determine if title insurance is possible
- ☑ Confirm the lot is buildable and legal (not merged or restricted)

Case Study: The Triple Lien Flip, Cleveland, OH

Scenario: Investor finds a property on the demolition list. Title shows:

- Deceased owner
- $13K demo lien
- $9K in unpaid utilities
- Multiple heirs in three different states

Action Taken:

- Contacted heirs using obituary + social
- Paid each $1,000 to sign a quitclaim
- Negotiated demo lien to $4,000
- Cleared utility balance with $2,000 settlement
- Filed Quiet Title
- Resold lot to a builder with plans for $58,000

Total All-In: $12,700
Net Profit: $45,300
Timeline: 6 months

Tools: Legal Documents You'll Use Often

- Quitclaim Deed Template (Universal Use)
- Affidavit of Heirship
- Demolition Lien Payoff Request Letter
- Sample Court Petition (Stay or Quiet Title)

- Zoning Confirmation Request

Keep these templates editable. You'll reuse them frequently.

Investor Fast Track Recap

- Always begin with a title search and lien check
- Don't fear inherited properties, solve them with documents, not drama
- Cities will negotiate demo liens, especially if you have plans
- Court intervention is powerful. Be present as a problem-solver, not a flipper
- Keep legal templates organized, editable, and signed by licensed pros

Chapter 4: Evaluating Demolition Properties for Profit Potential

Quick Start Summary

Not all condemned or fire-damaged properties are the same. Some will yield six-figure profits; others will drain your capital and bury you in bureaucratic red tape. This chapter arms you with a clear, step-by-step methodology to evaluate a demolition property's true potential. You'll learn how to assess zoning, market demand, demo cost, rebuild strategy, and end-user value so you never waste time on a losing deal. When dealing with a used properly, this evaluation framework becomes your investment filter, your risk-reduction tool, and your competitive edge.

The Core Mindset: Think Like a Developer

To win in demolition real estate, you must stop thinking like a flipper and start thinking like a developer.

A flipper looks at cosmetic repairs. A developer looks at **land utility, zoning overlays,** and **highest-and-best use**.

Demolition properties aren't about restoring old structures; they're about **unlocking the full potential of the dirt beneath them.**

So when evaluating a property, your first question is not, *"Can I save this structure?"* it's, *"Is this lot worth controlling, clearing, and rebuilding on?"*

7-Factor Evaluation Framework

Factor 1: Lot Value & Location

Use land comps to determine if the lot alone justifies your investment. Infill neighborhoods, high-demand zip codes, and areas with active redevelopment are ideal.

Target: Lots that resell for $25K-$75K+ post-demo

Factor 2: Zoning & Buildability

Check zoning codes to determine what can be built on the lot:

- Single-family
- Duplex or ADU
- Mixed-use
- Minimum lot width & depth

Warning: Many condemned lots are non-conforming and will require zoning variances to rebuild.

Factor 3: Existing Structure Condition

If the property is only 40-50% damaged, you may consider saving the foundation or framing. If damage exceeds 70%, full demolition is often more efficient.

Condition	Action
Foundation solid, no char.	Retain slab
Walls bowing or fire-damaged	Full demo
Utilities intact	Lower site prep cost

Factor 4: Demo Cost

Get estimates from 2-3 demo contractors. Typical residential demo costs range from **$8,000-$25,000**, depending on:

- Square footage
- Asbestos or lead removal
- Disposal fees
- Access issues (tight urban lots)

Factor 5: Environmental Issues

Lead paint, asbestos, underground oil tanks, or mold can drive up demo costs. Always verify:

- Year built (pre-1978 = lead risk)
- Local asbestos abatement laws
- Underground tanks with site inspection

Factor 6: Utility Access

A buildable lot must have access to:

- Sewer or septic
- Water
- Electric
- Gas (optional, depending on market). *If utilities are cut at the street or capped, get tap-in quotes before buying.*

Factor 7: Exit Strategy Alignment

Every evaluation ends with one key question: Does this property align with my exit strategy—build to flip, hold for rent, or sell the lot?

If the numbers and site logistics don't support that strategy, **walk away,** no matter how cheap the acquisition price.

Visual Evaluation: The Drive-by Test

When scouting properties, your eyes will reveal a lot. Bring your smartphone or drone for photos.

Visual Cue	What It Tells You
Caution tape / boarded windows	Active code enforcement
Overgrowth + no meter	Vacant > 2 years
Roof caved in / tilted	Demo required
Street active with new builds	Strong resale demand
Abandoned vehicles	Potential for city lien or environmental hazard

Document these signs in your deal tracker and take note of neighboring conditions.

Case Study: 90 Days to $40K Profit

Location: Pittsburgh, PA
Property: Fire-damaged duplex
Lot Size: 38' x 120'
Purchase Price: $6,500
Demo Cost: $14,800
Environmental: Required asbestos clearance

Utilities: Sewer + electric intact
Exit Strategy: Flip cleared lot to the builder

Action Taken:

- Secured demo permit
- Hired licensed crew
- Cleared lot and graded
- Packaged site with modular builder estimate
- Sold lot for $63,000 to investor targeting new construction

Net Profit: $41,700
Timeline: 94 days
Lesson: Evaluation + speed = scalable results

The Demolition Evaluation Scorecard

Use this scorecard to quickly rate a property before committing:

Factor	Score (1–10)	Notes
Lot Value Potential	9	$70K comps nearby
Zoning Flexibility	7	Duplex allowed by right
Damage Severity	4	Structure 80% burned
Demo Cost Estimate	6	$12–15K estimated
Environmental Risk	8	No asbestos or tanks
Utility Access	5	Sewer and electric verified
Exit Strategy Match	9	Lot sale to builder feasible
Total Score	**48/70**	*Strong Greenlight*

Common Red Flags to Avoid

- **Lot too narrow to build** (often <25' wide in urban zones)
- **Buried tanks or toxic materials** (expensive cleanup)
- **No legal access to the property** (landlocked lots)
- **Historic district restrictions** (demo prohibited)
- **Sloped or flood zone land** (engineering costs explode)

When in doubt, consult zoning, order a site survey, and walk the property.

Investor Fast Track Recap

- Evaluate every deal through the 7-Factor Lens: location, zoning, structure, demo, environmental, utilities, and exit
- Use your scorecard and visual walkthrough to reduce risk
- Never buy because it's cheap; buy only if it's **buildable and bankable**
- Validate demand and comps *before* you spend on demo
- Pass on projects that don't clearly align with your model

Chapter 5: Negotiating With Owners and Municipalities: Securing the Deal Before the Bulldozer

Quick Start Summary

Demolition deals are rarely listed. That means you're either negotiating directly with distressed owners or working with government agencies to access forfeited, condemned, or land bank properties. This chapter teaches you how to approach both. You'll get scripts, offer structures, legal tools, and psychological tactics that get deals done. Master this skill, and you'll consistently acquire properties before they hit auction, demolition, or market exposure.

The Two-Track Approach: Owner vs. City

There are only two ways into a demolition property:

1. **Owner-Directed Acquisition**: You find the individual (or heirs) who hold title and get them to sell it to you—often for pennies—simply for a chance to walk away from risk and liability.
2. **Municipal Acquisition or Intervention**: You acquire or take control of the property via court approval, land bank programs, or lien foreclosure, usually because no private party is actively defending the asset.

To scale this business, you'll need to become fluent in both.

Negotiating with Distressed or Absent Owners

Understand the Seller's Psychology

Demolition property owners often feel:

- **Embarrassed** by the condition of the home
- **Afraid** of city fines, lawsuits, or code enforcement
- **Overwhelmed** by legal obligations
- **Disconnected** from the asset (especially if it was inherited)

Your job is to be calm, competent, and solution-oriented.

Sample Outreach Script (Phone or Door)

"Hi, is this [Owner Name]? I'm calling about a property that may still be in your name at [Address]. I specialize in acquiring properties that need major repair or are at risk of demolition. I'd like to help resolve any city issues, and I'm prepared to take care of the paperwork and costs. Would you be open to a brief conversation?"

Sample Letter (Mailed or Dropped at Door)

Dear [Name],

I'm reaching out about [Address]. As you may know, this property has been cited for demolition by the city. I help owners by taking over properties like this, resolving any liens, and preventing further legal action.

I'm offering a fast, hassle-free solution and will pay all legal and closing costs. You won't owe the city a dime.

Please contact me at [Phone] or [Email] if you're open to a conversation.

Respectfully,
[Your Name]
[Your LLC or Entity Name]

Structuring the Offer

Here's a simple offer framework that wins trust:

Term	Description
Purchase Price	Usually $500-$5,000 (depending on value and risk)
Closing Costs	You pay 100%
Lien Assumption	You cover known municipal liens (e.g., demo or water bills)
Legal Paperwork	You handle all title transfers, notary, and court filings
Quick Close	Offer 14 days or less to close in cash

Always use a **Quitclaim Deed + Purchase Agreement** (or full title closing if required for future resale).

Acquiring from Municipalities

When a property has been:

- Forfeited to the land bank
- Abandoned and condemned
- Past due on taxes for 3+ years
- Already demolished

…the city may now control the asset. You can still acquire it, but you must present a professional, compliance-ready plan.

What the City Wants to See

Item	Purpose
Redevelopment Plan	How you'll use the property (build, sell, rent)
Proof of Funds	Bank statement or lender letter
Rehab Timeline	Detailed calendar (30/60/90-day milestones)
Licensed Contractor Letter	Who will perform the work
Past Project Photos	Credibility booster
Site Plan or Rendering	Visual idea of future outcome

Most land banks have an application process. Make sure you submit yours professionally.

Case Study: The $1 Property Flip, Buffalo, NY

Scenario: Investor contacted the Buffalo Land Bank to inquire about properties in zip codes with increasing construction permits.

Action Taken:

- Submitted application with builder partnership
- Acquired two demolished lots for $1 each
- Added renderings + utility confirmations
- Flipped to modular builder for $41,000 total

Timeline: 60 days

Total Cost: $1,650 (incl. fees)
Net Profit: $39,350
Lesson: Cities want builders, not speculators, so show your plan and move fast.

Overcoming Objections from Owners or Officials

Objection	Response
"I'm not sure I want to sell"	"I completely understand. I'm simply offering a stress-free solution to avoid future fines or legal costs."
"There are too many liens"	"I've worked with the city before. I can negotiate or settle liens on your behalf and handle all the paperwork."
"The city's already scheduled demo"	"That's okay. I can request a stay from the court and present a redevelopment plan."
"I don't trust people with these kinds of offers"	"Understood. I'm a licensed business owner. We'll use legal documents, and I'll pay all costs through a title company if needed."

Templates to Use

- Demolition Property Purchase Agreement
- Owner Lien Waiver Acknowledgment Form
- Municipal Proposal Template (Redevelopment Plan)
- City Meeting Talking Points
- Land Bank Application Checklist

Keep these loaded in your CRM or deal kit. They save hours per lead.

Investor Fast Track Recap

- Demolition deals happen **before the listing**—by calling heirs, owners, and city departments
- Approach owners with **compassion, clarity,** and a **solution**
- Offer to handle **everything**: liens, legal, and logistics
- Present cities with **plans and credibility.** They don't want speculation

- Use the right templates and track every contact, you'll close more than you miss

Chapter 6: Court & Municipal Release Processes: Unlocking Properties Stuck in the System

Quick Start Summary

Many of the most profitable demolition deals are locked behind bureaucracy: court orders, condemnation notices, title clouds, and active demolition schedules. But what most investors don't know is that **you can intervene, delay** or **stop demolition,** and even **petition for release or reassignment of property rights.** In this chapter, you'll learn the legal and administrative processes that allow you to reclaim properties others assume are already lost, and how to present yourself as a credible, capable solution provider to the city, courts, and public administrators.

Why Properties Get Stuck and Why That's Your Opportunity

Cities don't want to own property. They don't want to demolish buildings. And they certainly don't want legal exposure from condemned structures or vacant homes attracting crime.

But when:

- An owner dies without a will
- Heirs abandon the asset
- A building is fire-damaged and left unattended
- A nuisance case escalates into court
- Or the city pays to demolish it and recoup via liens

That property becomes an orphan: Stuck in the system, without an advocate.

Enter *you*: The investor who understands the legal process and knows how to take responsibility before it's too late.

Demolition Orders: How They Work

Demolition Order Types

Type	Description
Emergency Demo	Building poses an immediate threat to life—no appeal possible.
Standard Demo	Issued due to prolonged code violations—can often be paused.
Judicial Demo	Court-ordered tear-down—requires a legal motion to intervene.

Your job is to identify demo orders that are not yet enforced and intervene with a plan.

How to Stop a Scheduled Demolition

Yes, you can stop (or delay) a demolition, even when the order is already issued.

Step-by-Step Guide to Filing a Demo Stay:

1. **Obtain the case file**
   - Visit the housing or municipal court clerk
   - Ask for all filings related to the address
   - Review condemnation orders and lien history
2. **Draft a Petition to Stay Demolition**
   - Include your name or entity as an interested buyer
   - State that you intend to acquire and bring the property into compliance
   - Outline your timeline, contractor letter, and financial capability
3. **Attach Supporting Docs**
   - Copy of signed purchase agreement or quitclaim intent
   - Contractor bid or rehab budget
   - Photos, insurance certificate, and site plan (if possible)
4. **File the Motion in Court**
   - Pay the nominal court fee ($30-$100)
   - Schedule a hearing (typically within 7-14 days)

    - Be ready to speak or provide testimony on your plans
5. **Appear or Submit via Attorney**
    - Be professional, respectful, and organized
    - Emphasize community benefit, compliance, and quick resolution

Sample Petition Excerpt

IN THE MUNICIPAL COURT OF [County]

Re: Request to Stay Demolition – 733 N. Glendale Ave.

I, Calyn Smart, on behalf of [Your LLC Name], respectfully petition the court to delay or stay the scheduled demolition of the above-referenced property.

I am currently under contract to acquire the property, have obtained a rehabilitation bid from [Licensed Contractor Name], and am prepared to resolve all violations within 90 days.

Attached are:

- Signed agreement of sale
- Licensed contractor letter of intent
- Photo evidence
- Estimated budget
- Compliance timeline

We believe demolition is unnecessary and counterproductive to the City's revitalization goals and respectfully request this opportunity to restore the site.

Sincerely,
[Signature]
[Contact Info]

How to Work with the City, Not Against It

Most investors are afraid of City Hall. That's a mistake.

City employees are overworked and overloaded. What they want is:

- A plan
- A responsible party

- A track record
- A fast, legal resolution

How to Present Yourself to Officials:

- Call or visit the Code Enforcement Director, Land Bank Manager, or Housing Department
- Introduce yourself and your company as a Blight Solutions partner
- Say clearly: "I'm here to reclaim and redevelop problem properties before they get demolished or lost."
- Bring examples of your past work
- Ask how you can help relieve their caseload

Most cities have policies to **pause** or **cancel demolition** if an investor steps in with legal control and compliance intent.

Acquiring Properties Post-demo

If a property has already been demolished, it still has value—as land.

Here's how to acquire it:

Option A: Land Bank or Municipal Sale

- City may hold title after tax foreclosure or demolition
- Submit a proposal with a plan, builder, timeline, and project cost
- Many sell lots for $1-$10,000 with redevelopment clauses

Option B: Lien Redemption

- City placed a lien but hasn't foreclosed
- You can negotiate lien reduction and acquire the deed from the owner
- Then build or sell as a cleared lot

Option C: Judicial Foreclosure

- You initiate legal foreclosure on a property where you hold lien (as a contractor, tax buyer, or investor)
- Gain deed through court and wipe clean all subordinate liens

Case Study: The Courtroom Save, Milwaukee, WI

Background: A two-flat had been fire-damaged and condemned for over two years. The city scheduled a demo for March 1. The investor filed a stay on February 17 with full plan and support docs.

What Happened:

- Judge granted a 60-day stay
- Investor acquired via quitclaim for $1,500
- Paid $14K for demo
- Sold the cleared lot for $33,000 with city-approved plans

Result:

- Timeline: 74 days
- Net Profit: $15,000
- Cost avoided: City demo fee + forced teardown
- Impact: Preserved legal title and leveraged early action

Court & City Contact Strategy

Step	Who to Contact	Purpose
Before demo is filed	Code Enforcement	Prevent formal notice
Demo ordered but not executed	Housing Court Clerk	File motion to stay
Post-demo	Land Bank or Planning Dept	Submit proposal
In case of lien	Treasurer's Office	Request a payoff and negotiate
For title acquisition	Real Estate Division / Legal	Verify the ownership transfer process

Templates & Tools for Intervention

- Petition to Stay Demolition (Fillable PDF)
- City Partnership Presentation (PowerPoint)
- Contractor Letter of Intent (Editable Doc)
- Land Bank Application Template
- Court Appearance Preparation Checklist

Investor Fast Track Recap

- Demolition orders are often pauseable, negotiable, and reversible
- Present the court and city with a solution, not a plea
- Legal ownership + compliance plan = powerful leverage
- Acquire lots post-demo for land value and build equity from scratch
- Keep templates, timelines, and proof of intent ready at all times

Chapter 7: Permits, Liens & Legal Hurdles: Clearing the Path to Profit

Quick Start Summary

Demolition investing requires more than vision. It requires navigation.

You'll encounter unpaid liens, complex permit requirements, legal obligations, and hidden restrictions that can stall your project and kill your ROI. But armed with the right knowledge, documents, and preparation, you can streamline the approval process, negotiate debt, and eliminate the most common deal-killing hurdles before they stop you.

This chapter gives you a practical roadmap to secure permits, reduce liabilities, and move from demolition to development with control and confidence.

The Reality of Red Tape

Every city has one thing in common: Bureaucracy.

When you buy a standard house, your biggest concern is the seller's disclosure. But when you're dealing with a condemned or demolished property, you may be dealing with:

- Unpaid water bills
- Demo liens
- Code enforcement fines
- Open violations
- Permit denials
- Zoning conflicts
- Environmental clearance requirements

And here's the hard truth: You are responsible for all of it once you become the legal owner.

That's why this chapter exists—to help you identify, understand, and clear these issues upfront.

Types of Liens You Must Understand

1. **Demolition Lien**
   - Issued when a city pays to demolish a structure, places the bill on the property
   - Can range from $8,000 to $30,000+
   - Must be satisfied before resale or development
2. **Utility Liens**
   - Water, sewer, and sometimes trash services can attach to the property, not the person
   - Some cities do not extinguish these liens upon tax sale
3. **Code Enforcement Fines**
   - Nuisance abatement, lawn mowing, boarding-up windows
   - Often cumulative and silently compounding
4. **Environmental Liens**
   - Issued if the property required hazmat response or cleanup (e.g., asbestos, illegal dumping)
   - May involve state or federal agencies

Most of these are negotiable. Cities are often willing to settle liens for pennies on the dollar if you demonstrate intent to redevelop.

How to Request a Lien Payoff or Reduction

Steps:

1. Contact the Treasurer's office or Building Department
2. Request a Lien Payoff Statement (in writing)
3. If purchasing the property, attach a Letter of Intent or Purchase Agreement
4. Offer a settlement amount (typically 30–60% of the total)
5. Submit a Redevelopment Plan as justification
6. Request a Lien Release Letter upon acceptance

Cities want blight removed. Offering to turn a vacant lot into a livable property makes your offer more attractive than litigation or foreclosure.

Sample Lien Payoff Request Letter:

To: City Treasurer – Liens Department
From: [Your LLC Name]
Re: Request for Lien Payoff and Settlement – 2042 West Pierce Avenue

Dear [Name],

I am writing to formally request a lien payoff statement for the above-referenced property, which we are under contract to purchase.

We understand the city has incurred demolition and nuisance-related costs. We are preparing a redevelopment plan for the site and are requesting consideration for a lien reduction in light of our intent to bring the lot back into productive use.

Attached:

- Copy of signed purchase agreement
- Contractor letter of intent
- Site improvement timeline

We are offering $7,500 in satisfaction of the listed balances, conditional upon title transfer and site approval.

Sincerely,
[Your Name]
[Your Phone & Email]

Understanding Permits in Demolition Investing

Unlike rehabs, teardown properties require **a new set of permits**, even if you're only clearing the land.

Required Permits May Include:

Permit Type	Purpose
Demolition Permit	Legal permission to remove structure
Sewer Cap / Disconnect	Properly close water/sewer lines
Utility Disconnects	Electric, gas, and water shutdown
Site Grading / Fill	Smooth the land post-demo
Asbestos Clearance	If structure contains hazardous materials
Building Permit	New construction approval
Zoning Variance	Needed if lot is non-conforming
Curb Cut / Driveway Permit	If modifying entry to the lot

Start early. Some cities take 2-3 months to approve building permits or zoning variances.

Permit Roadblocks and How to Avoid Them

Roadblock: Lot is too small for zoning

Solution:

- Request zoning variance
- Combine with neighboring parcel
- Shift design to modular or skinny-home build

Roadblock 01: Permits denied due to previous violations

Solution:

- Present compliance plan
- Pay outstanding fines
- Request "reset" inspection post-clearance

Roadblock 01: City won't issue permits until liens are paid

Solution:

- Negotiate lien settlement
- Offer lien payment escrow
- Include lien resolution clause in purchase agreement

Environmental and Legal Hurdles

Many demolition sites contain environmental risks like:

- Lead-based paint
- Asbestos siding
- Underground oil tanks
- Illegal dumping
- Soil contamination

If identified:

- Hire a licensed environmental inspector
- Get a Phase I Environmental Site Assessment
- Obtain clearance certificates before proceeding

Some cities offer **brownfield grants** or environmental tax credits to offset remediation costs.

Case Study: Clearing a $27K Lien for $5,200, St. Louis, MO

An investor acquired a vacant lot that had been demoed two years earlier. It carried a $27,000 lien for demolition, fencing, and emergency hazmat removal.

Strategy:

- Presented the city with an infill modular housing plan
- Attached contractor quotes and proof of funding
- Negotiated a $5,200 settlement
- Paid via escrow and recorded lien release
- Cleared title and sold to builder for $47,000

Net Profit: $27,800
Lesson: Cities are often more flexible than assumed, especially when you show them what they stand to gain.

Templates and Documents You'll Need

- Lien Payoff Request Letter
- Demolition Permit Application
- Contractor Disconnect Affidavit
- Grading Permit Worksheet
- Asbestos Inspection Checklist
- Environmental Clearance Certificate
- Zoning Confirmation Request Letter
- Escrow Agreement for Conditional Permit

Investor Fast Track Recap

- Expect liens—don't fear them. Most are **negotiable**.
- Secure permits **before** planning your exit strategy.
- Always check for environmental hazards and lead-based risks.
- Use official letters, full plans, and documentation to negotiate in your favor.
- Keep a digital folder of all required forms and city contacts for each region you invest in.

Chapter 8: Planning Your Project: From Demo to Development

Quick Start Summary

Once a demolition site is cleared, the real work begins.

Whether you intend to build new construction, flip the land, or create long-term rental assets, a strategic and well-scoped development plan is essential.

This chapter guides you through everything you need to transform a cleared lot into a high-value, profitable asset. From selecting the right build type, creating architectural plans, obtaining approvals, and managing the budget, this is your roadmap to transforming demolition into development wealth.

From Rubble to Revenue: Thinking Like a Builder

A cleared lot is not an endpoint; it's a blank canvas.

The question is: *What should be built here, and who will pay for it?*

Great developers don't start with bricks. They start with questions:

- Who's buying in this neighborhood?
- What's missing in the market?
- What can I legally build here?
- What design will maximize value on this lot?

Whether your exit strategy is flip, hold, or JV (joint venture), your project plan should begin with **demand**, not just square footage.

Three Post-Demo Strategies to Consider

Option 01: Build to Flip

You clear the lot, build new construction, and sell the finished home.

Ideal when:

- High comp values in the neighborhood
- Strong retail buyer demand
- You have construction funding or partner access

Option 02: Build to Hold

You build a rental-ready asset—single-family, duplex, or ADU—and refinance after completion.

Ideal when:

- Low property taxes
- Area supports stable rents
- Your goal is long-term cash flow

Option 03: Flip the Lot

You clear the lot, prep a builder-ready package, and sell the land.

Ideal When:

- You don't want construction risk
- Lot value is already high
- You can add value via zoning, renderings, or plans

Designing the Right Project

Step 01: Verify Zoning and Use

Before choosing a design, confirm:

- Allowed building type (single-family, duplex, multifamily, mixed-use)
- Minimum lot size
- Setbacks, height limits, and parking requirements
- Floodplain or historic district restrictions
- Occupancy type (residential vs. commercial)

Use a **Zoning Confirmation Letter** from your local Planning Office if necessary.

Step 02: Choose Your Build Type

Build Type	Cost Range (psf)	Build Time	Notes
Stick-Built	$130-$220	5-9 months	Fully customizable, higher cost

Modular	$95-$140	3-5 months	Factory-built, faster ROI
Prefab Panels	$100-$160	4-6 months	Hybrid of stick/modular
Container or Tiny Home	$75-$110	2-3 months	Niche appeal, zoning-sensitive

Modular builds allow scalability and fixed pricing—excellent for infill and urban lots.

Key Team Members and Roles

Role	Responsibility
Architect / Draftsman	Site plan, floor plans, elevation drawings
General Contractor (GC)	Manages labor, materials, and inspections
Civil Engineer	Required for grading, drainage, or complex sites
Real Estate Attorney	Reviews contracts, permits, and compliance
Project Manager (optional)	Oversees schedules and budget

Start with experienced professionals familiar with **urban infill** or **demo-to-new construction**.

Budgeting the Project

Use this basic formula to create your build plan:

All-In Cost = Lot + Demo + Site Prep + Build + Permits + Holding

Sample Budget (3BR Modular – Urban Lot)

Item	Amount
Lot Cost	$12,000

Demo	$14,000
Site Prep	$8,500
Modular Build (1,400 sf @ $110/sf)	$154,000
Permits & Fees	$9,000
Utilities / Tap Fees	$11,500
Holding Costs (6 months)	$6,000
Contingency (10%)	$21,500
Total	**$236,500**

Target ARV: $310,000
Projected Profit (Pre-Tax): $73,500
Timeline: 5-6 months

Visual Project Planning Tools

Use a Gantt chart or online dashboard (Trello, ClickUp, or

Phase	Duration	Key Task
Pre-Construction	4-6 weeks	Design, permits, contracts
Demo & Site Prep	1-2 weeks	Clearing, grading, utility cuts
Foundation & Framing	2-4 weeks	Modular install or stick framing
Systems (MEP)	2-3 weeks	Mechanical, Electrical, Plumbing
Finishes & Final Walkthrough	3-5 weeks	Interior, paint, landscaping
Listing / Lease-Up	1–3 weeks	Photos, staging, showings

Monday.com) to map the project by weeks and phases:

Case Study: From Fire Lot to Modern Duplex, Atlanta, GA

Background:
An investor acquired a fire-damaged property in a transitioning neighborhood. Paid $8,000 for the structure.

Demo cost: $16,000.

They cleared the site and engaged a modular builder for a 2-unit duplex.

Total Build: $278,000
ARV (Appraised): $398,000
Exit: Rented for $2,900/month → refinanced 75% LTV
Cash Out: $298,500
Profit + Long-Term Asset: Yes

Lesson: Clear vision + clean execution = scalable income.

Must-have Documents and Plans

- Site Plan + Floor Plan
- Elevation Drawing
- Utility Map + Tap-In Requests
- Grading & Soil Report
- Scope of Work (GC Contract)
- Draw Schedule (Payment Milestones)
- Permit Packet (Demo + Build)
- Builder's Insurance Certificate

Keep all documents in cloud folders for quick access for lenders, inspectors, and city officials.

Investor Fast-Track Recap

- Begin with demand and design backward—build what sells, not what's easy
- Choose modular or stick based on zoning, speed, and capital
- Use professional plans and packages to unlock permits quickly
- Budget for everything: demo, prep, permits, and contingency
- Track progress with visual tools and professional documentation

Chapter 9: Managing the Demolition Process: Clearing the Land Without Losing Control

Quick Start Summary

Demolition is the bridge between acquiring a distressed property and executing a profitable development. It's also one of the most misunderstood and poorly managed phases by new investors.

This chapter will guide you through each step of the demolition process, from selecting the right contractor and obtaining permits to handling environmental compliance, inspections, and post-demo grading.

When managed correctly, demolition becomes your clean slate, a springboard to profitable redevelopment. When mismanaged, it becomes a delay-filled, budget-draining liability.

Why Professional Demolition Matters

You're not just knocking down a building; you're setting the stage for what comes next.

A poorly handled demolition can:

- Delay your permit process
- Trigger fines or code violations
- Expose you to lawsuits (e.g., improper disposal, worker injury)
- Jeopardize your build timeline
- Drive your budget over by 25-40%

A well-managed demo:

- Prepares the site to exact city standards
- Minimizes liability and delays
- Increases property value
- Builds credibility with local agencies and contractors

Before You Begin: Pre-Demo Checklist

Before hiring equipment or swinging hammers, ensure the following:

Task	Status
☐ Demolition Permit Issued	From city/county building department
☐ Utility Disconnects Scheduled	Electric, gas, water, sewer
☐ Asbestos / Lead Paint Tested	Required in many cities
☐ Structural Engineer Report (optional)	If property has partial salvage value
☐ Neighbor Notification (if required)	For attached or shared-wall structures
☐ Insurance Certificate (from contractor)	Liability + workers comp
☐ Site Fence / Signage Installed	Required in most jurisdictions
☐ Environmental Clearance Documentation	EPA or local authority requirements

Start the permit and disconnect process as soon as you acquire the property; it often takes 2-4 weeks.

Selecting the Right Demolition Contractor

Choose a licensed, insured, and experienced contractor who:

- Has completed 10+ residential teardowns
- Is familiar with local permitting and disposal laws
- Provides full-service handling: permit pulling, teardown, debris haul-away, grading
- Can show references and previous site photos

Questions to Ask:

- Are you licensed and bonded in this city?
- Will you pull all required permits on my behalf?
- What does your quote include: disposal fees, backfill, inspections?
- Can you provide a start and completion date guarantee?
- Do you handle asbestos if found?

Never use a contractor who asks you to pull the permit under your name.

Demolition Cost Factors

Cost Component	Typical Range
Structure Size	\$4–\$10 per sq. ft.
Permit Fees	\$300–\$2,000
Asbestos Removal	\$3,000–\$20,000 (if needed)
Site Grading & Fill	\$1,500–\$6,000
Hauling & Disposal	\$2,000–\$10,000

Total Residential Demo: \$8,000-\$25,000+

Get 2-3 itemized quotes and compare scope, not just the price.

The Demolition Timeline

Phase	Duration	Notes
Permitting & Utility Disconnect	2-4 weeks	City backlogs are common
Site Prep (fencing, survey)	2-3 days	May require professional surveyor
Structure Tear-Down	1-3 days	Weather can delay
Debris Removal	2-5 days	Confirm dump site documentation
Grading & Final Inspection	3-7 days	Must meet city compaction standards

Total estimated duration: **3-6 weeks**, start to finish

Environmental Compliance & Safety

Cities and state agencies are highly sensitive to:

- Improper asbestos removal
- Illegal dumping
- Soil contamination

- Unauthorized burning or burying of material

To Stay Compliant:

- Require contractor to provide **disposal tickets** and **asbestos manifest**
- Use only **licensed abatement professionals** for hazardous materials
- Backfill only with **clean fill**, no construction debris or organic material
- Photograph the site before, during, and after work

Your liability doesn't end when the structure falls. If rules are broken, you can be held financially and legally responsible.

Final Inspection and Site Prep for Rebuilding

Once the structure is removed:

1. Call for **Final Inspection** from the building or code department
2. Confirm that the lot is **level, compacted,** and **free of debris**
3. Obtain the **Demolition Completion Certificate** or inspection pass slip
4. Store all receipts and inspection reports for lender or resale documentation
5. If building soon, stake lot corners and prepare for the next phase (foundation)

Take before and after photos to include in your build permit package.

Case Study: One-day Demo, Five-day Flip, Minneapolis, MN

Background: An investor acquired a boarded-up duplex in a pre-gentrification zip. Hired a demo contractor with city experience.

Timeline:

- Day 1: Utilities confirmed disconnected
- Day 2: Structure fully demolished
- Day 3-4: Debris cleared
- Day 5: Lot leveled and final inspection passed

Total Cost: $13,900
Result: Sold cleared lot 3 weeks later for $42,000 with plans included

Net Profit: $22,000
Lesson: Speed + cleanliness + documentation = fast cashout.

Demolition Toolkit: Templates & Contracts

- Demolition Contractor Agreement
- Permit Checklist Template
- Asbestos Abatement Notice Form
- Debris Hauling Manifest Log
- Pre- and Post-Demo Photo Log
- Final Inspection Approval Request
- Insurance & License Verification Sheet

Investor Fast-Track Recap

- Plan your demolition like a construction project—timeline, budget, and paperwork
- Hire professionals who know your market and permit office
- Always pre-inspect for asbestos and get full environmental clearance
- Track your process with forms and photos—your credibility depends on it
- Use the clean lot to launch your next stage—don't stall post-demo

Chapter 10: Construction & Rebuild Strategy: Turning Dirt into Dividends

Quick Start Summary

Once your demolition is complete, your cleared lot becomes a blank canvas, beaming with potential. But this next phase—construction or rebuild—is where many investors either scale to six figures or stumble into delays, overruns, and low-margin outcomes.

This chapter walks you through the rebuild process step by step: choosing between modular and stick-built construction, budgeting accurately, hiring and managing contractors, navigating inspections, and aligning your build with a profitable exit strategy.

This is where you turn your demolition deal into a wealth-building engine.

Choosing the Right Construction Strategy

Your first major decision is whether to build traditionally (stick-built) or use alternative construction methods like modular, prefab panels, or even container builds.

Stick-built Construction

- Built on site, piece by piece
- Most familiar to contractors, lenders, and appraisers
- Greater customization, but longer build times

Pros: Flexibility, traditional financing, and strong resale value
Cons: Longer timelines, more labor risk, and weather delays

Modular Construction

- Pre-built sections (modules) delivered and assembled on site
- Factory-controlled environment ensures quality and speed
- Ideal for infill and small urban lots

Pros: Faster build time, fewer subs to manage, and fixed cost
Cons: Upfront factory order payments and transportation logistics

In urban areas or areas with rising demand and zoning limits, modular builds provide speed and predictability, making them ideal for demo-to-rebuild plays.

The Construction Timeline: What to Expect

Phase	Duration (Stick-Built)	Duration (Modular)
Design & Permitting	30-60 days	30-45 days
Site Work & Foundation	2-3 weeks	2 weeks
Framing / Modular Delivery	4-6 weeks	1 week
MEP (Mechanical, Electrical, Plumbing)	2-3 weeks	1-2 weeks
Drywall, Finishes, Exterior	4-6 weeks	2-4 weeks
Inspections & CO	1-2 weeks	1 week

Total Build Time:

- Stick-Built: 4.5-7 months
- Modular: 2.5-4 months

Building Budget Breakdown

Let's assume a 3BR, 2BA home at 1,500 square feet.

Category	Stick-Built	Modular
Lot & Demo	$20,000	$20,000
Permits & Fees	$7,500	$7,500
Site Prep & Foundation	$14,000	$12,000
Build Cost	$195,000 ($130/sf)	$157,500 ($105/sf)
Utilities & Tap-Ins	$12,000	$12,000
Landscaping & Final Grading	$4,000	$3,000
Contingency (10-15%)	$25,000	$20,000

Total	$277,500	$232,000

Target resale value (ARV): $310,000-$340,000
Gross Margin: $60K-$90K, depending on construction path

Contractor Selection & Management

Vetting a General Contractor (GC)

- Check licenses, bonding, and insurance
- Ask for a portfolio of recent builds
- Confirm permit experience in your city
- Get line-item bids and compare apples to apples
- Require lien waivers and milestone-based payments

Contract Essentials

- Fixed price vs. cost-plus pricing
- Draw schedule tied to inspection milestones
- Start and finish dates (with penalties for delays)
- Scope of work attached
- Subcontractor approval clause

Build Oversight: Weekly Management Checklist

Task	Responsible Party	Notes
Confirm weekly progress vs. schedule	You / PM	Compare with Gantt chart
Verify inspections are passed	GC	Foundation, framing, rough MEP
Walk job site for quality control	You	Check for safety, cleanup
Approve or delay draw payment	You	Only after verified milestones
Communicate with lender (if applicable)	You	Submit progress reports

Consistency = Control.

Even if you're not swinging a hammer, your presence and documentation drive results.

Permits, Inspections & Certificate of Occupancy (CO)

Typical Inspections Required:

- Foundation/footings
- Framing
- Rough electrical, plumbing, and HVAC (MEP)
- Insulation
- Drywall
- Final building & safety

Each must be passed before proceeding to the next. Cities often require:

- Job site signage
- Permit displayed
- Dumpster & porta-potty on site
- Final CO for sale or occupancy

Keep a binder or Google Drive folder for all permits, passes, and inspection reports.

Case Study: Build to Flip, Cleveland, OH

Background:
An investor cleared a condemned duplex, subdivided the lot, and installed a 3BR/2BA modular on a 35-foot infill parcel.

Costs:

- Lot & Demo: $19,000
- Modular Build (1,450 sf): $142,000
- Site Work, Tap-ins, Permit Fees: $28,500
- Total: $189,500

Sold: $289,000 in 27 days
Profit: $99,500 gross
Timeline: 4.2 months from demo to closing

Lesson: Modular wins on speed + simplicity.

Visual Tools: Planning & Budgeting Dashboards

Use software to track:

- Cost-to-complete forecasting (Excel or Buildertrend)
- Gantt chart schedule (ClickUp or Trello)
- Draw schedule tracker
- Contractor scorecard for quality & responsiveness

Share access with your bookkeeper, project manager, and partners for transparency.

Rebuild Templates You'll Need

- Scope of Work Template
- General Contractor Agreement
- Modular Builder Specification Sheet
- Payment Draw Schedule
- Inspection Log Sheet
- Project Timeline Gantt Chart
- Certificate of Occupancy Checklist

Investor Fast-Track Recap

- Choose your build type wisely—modular vs. stick—depending on your timeline, capital, and zoning
- Budget realistically with contingency and permit costs in mind
- Hire licensed, experienced contractors who know your jurisdiction
- Manage weekly with tools, site visits, and milestone tracking
- Finish with full documentation and use your build as a portfolio piece to scale up

Chapter 11: Sell the Lot vs. Build to Flip: Strategic Exit Decisions After Demolition

Quick Start Summary

You've cleared the site, verified zoning, and potentially even created renderings or modular plans. Now… you face a pivotal question: *Should you sell the lot as-is or build and flip it for a higher return?*

This chapter unpacks the financial, strategic, and psychological considerations behind each exit strategy. You'll learn how to calculate risk-adjusted ROI, assess local market demand, and structure either option for maximum value.

Whether you're chasing speed, scale, or equity, this decision determines your timeline, your returns, and your growth trajectory.

Understanding the Value in the Lot

A lot—especially one that's been demo-cleared, graded, and legally buildable—is an asset.

If it's in a desirable location, surrounded by construction or within a developing corridor, the lot itself may have *developer value* without you needing to build anything.

Rule of Thumb: *If cleared lots are selling for >35% of the ARV of new homes in the area, consider selling the lot.*

Build to Flip: The Full Equity Strategy

What It Means:

You invest in the full construction of a new structure—home, duplex, etc.—on your cleared lot and sell it turnkey on the open market.

Benefits:

- Capture full ARV-based profit
- Demonstrates capability (great for portfolio & lender credibility)
- Strongest ROI in appreciating markets

Risks:

- Timeline delays
- Construction overruns
- Interest carry (if using financing)
- Market softening before sale

Sell the Lot: The Velocity Strategy

What It Means:

You package the lot for a builder, developer, or investor—plans, surveys, renderings, and possibly permits—and sell it.

Benefits:

- Quick exit (often within 30-60 days)
- Minimal additional capital required
- Reduces holding risk
- Lets you recycle profits faster into the next deal

Risks:

- Lower gross profit
- Smaller buyer pool (especially for infill lots)
- City restrictions on who can purchase/what can be built

Decision Matrix: Sell vs. Build

Criteria	Sell the Lot	Build to Flip
Time to Exit	Fast (1-3 months)	Slow (4-9 months)
Risk Profile	Low	Medium–High
Capital Needed	Low (Post-demo only)	High (Full build cost)
Return	20-60%	30-100%+
Best In	Hot infill markets	Upward trending zip codes
Exit Buyer	Builders or investors	End buyers (retail)

Use your cost-to-value ratio to decide.

If your demo + holding cost is <25% of ARV, and you can build for <50%, you may want to build and flip.

If the lot value already equals 35-40% of ARV, selling may be the smarter short-term move.

Case Study 01: Lot Flip Win, Philadelphia, PA

Background: An investor purchased a condemned duplex for $8,000. Paid $14,500 for demo and grading. Paid $2,000 for site survey and $850 for architectural renderings.

All-In: $25,350
Sold Lot: $56,000 to builder 2 blocks from major redevelopment corridor
Timeline: 51 days
Net Profit: $30,650
Lesson: Plans + presentation = leverage. The investor never picked up a hammer but made a 120% return in under two months.

Case Study 02: Build-to-Flip Home Run, Houston, TX

Background: An investor cleared a fire-lot purchased for $9,000. Built a 3BR/2BA 1,500-sq-ft modular home for $169,000 (all in, including tap-ins, permits, holding).

Sold for: $289,000 to an FHA buyer
Total Timeline: 6.5 months
Gross Profit: ~$111,000
Lesson: For investors with build funding and project control, a full flip can deliver 2-3x the return of a lot sale, if the market holds steady.

How to Package a Lot for Sale

If you choose to sell the lot, make it irresistible to your buyer:

Asset	Why It Matters
Site Survey	Confirms legal boundaries & buildability
Zoning Verification Letter	Reduces buyer uncertainty
Soil Test (optional)	Speeds up builder decision

Renderings or Floor Plans	Helps buyer visualize value
Demo Receipts & Permit	Shows cleared title and readiness
Utility Map	Confirms tap-in access

Create a digital folder (PDF + links) you can send with every offer.

Lot Listing Strategy: Where to Sell

- MLS (via flat-fee listing agent)
- LandWatch / LotNetwork / LandFlip
- Facebook investor groups (by city)
- Local builder forums or chamber directories
- Direct emails to builders and developers in your region
- Offer seller-financing to expand buyer pool

Tip: *Add a sign on the lot with a QR code to your info pack, especially in active construction zones.*

Partner Strategy: Lot + Builder Split

Instead of selling or building solo, consider a **50/50 joint venture**:

- You provide the land, clear title, and demo
- Builder provides labor, materials, and permit management
- Profits split after sale

Benefits:

- No build capital required
- Profit > lot sale
- Retain skin in the game

Caution: Use a clear operating agreement + profit split agreement + exit timeline.

Templates You'll Need

- Lot Sale Enhancement Checklist
- Builder-Ready Marketing Packet (Template)
- Lot Listing Description Samples
- JV Agreement Template (Builder Partnership)

- Profit Comparison Calculator (Sell vs. Build)

Investor Fast-Track Recap

- Your cleared lot is an asset—choose your exit wisely
- Sell for speed and simplicity, build for equity and long-term growth
- Package lots with documents and visuals to maximize value
- Use decision metrics: lot % of ARV, construction cost, market trend
- Consider hybrid exit (builder JV or modular partnership) to balance risk and reward

Chapter 12: Marketing Your Final Product: Positioning, Packaging, and Selling with Authority

Quick Start Summary

Marketing is more than making noise; it's making value visible.

Whether you're selling a cleared lot, a new construction build, or a demo-ready parcel with plans, how you present your final product determines how quickly it sells and at what price.

This chapter shows you how to craft a strategic, compelling, and professional marketing package that attracts serious buyers, builds trust, and generates action. From listing platforms and professional visuals to direct outreach and builder targeting, you'll learn how to exit cleanly—and profitably.

What Are You Really Selling?

You're not selling dirt. You're selling **a vision**.

Whether it's a cleared lot, a finished home, or a permitted modular build site, your job is to present **certainty** in a market filled with risk.

What buyers want to know:

- Can I build or use this property without problems?
- Is the paperwork clean?
- Is this worth my time and capital?
- Can I see the result before I commit?

When you eliminate uncertainty, you multiply demand.

Core Marketing Assets to Build Trust

Asset	Description
High-Quality Photos	Professional shots of lot, structure, neighborhood

Drone Footage (optional)	Aerial views showcasing lot dimensions and nearby development
Site Survey	Shows boundary lines and legal buildability
Zoning Letter	Confirms allowable use (e.g., duplex, modular)
Renderings / Floor Plans	Visualizes what can be built
Demolition & Environmental Docs	Proves site is clean and ready
Utilities Map	Confirms access to water, sewer, electric, gas

Bundle all of this into a polished PDF or digital folder with labeled sections and download links.

Writing a Magnetic Listing Description

Your listing should be short, visual, and confidence-building.

Sample (Lot Sale):

Cleared, Buildable Lot in Active Redevelopment Zone!

Ready-to-build lot on a quiet block, just steps from new construction. All utilities available at the street.

- 40' x 125' lot size
- Zoned R-3 – allows single or 2-unit builds
- Site survey and demo permit included
- Clean title – ready for fast close
- Ideal for builder or investor

Includes 3BR/2BA modular rendering and city-confirmed utility access.

Contact for full info pack and walk-through appointment.

Asking: $49,000

Where to List: Best Platforms by Product Type

Product	Platforms
Cleared Lot	LandWatch, MLS (via flat-fee agent), Facebook Marketplace, LotNetwork
New Construction Build	Zillow, Redfin, Realtor.com, local MLS, new build directories
Permitted Site or Builder-Ready Package	Local builder groups, investor email lists, BiggerPockets, direct outreach

Bonus Strategy: Find 10 local builders and email your package directly. Builders love plug-and-play deals.

Retail Strategy: Marketing to End Buyers

If you're selling a finished property to a homeowner or an FHA buyer:

- Stage the property or use virtual staging
- Emphasize **warranty, energy efficiency,** and **brand-new systems**
- Highlight savings vs. older homes (e.g., HVAC, roof, plumbing)

Invest in:

- Wide-angle interior photography
- Twilight exterior shots
- "New construction" signage on property

List during peak buying season (Spring/Summer) to maximize price.

Lot or Site Sales: Marketing to Builders

Builder buyers are focused on:

- Timeline
- Permits
- Utility access
- Buildability
- Zoning

Create a "Builder Buyer Packet" with:

- Photos, site map, survey
- City zoning confirmation
- Cost to build estimate (if available)
- Nearby comps of new builds
- Incentives (e.g., seller financing or fast close discount)

Email & Direct Outreach Strategy

Create a simple message like:

Subject: Builder-Ready Lot – Permits, Survey & Plans Included

Hey [Name],

I have a buildable infill lot in [Neighborhood] with all paperwork complete: demo done, zoning confirmed, utility map, and 3BR floor plan.

Great opportunity to drop in a modular or stick-built home with strong comps.

Asking $52,000. Can send full packet if interested.

– Calyn

Attach your marketing one-pager or PDF folder

Case Study: Visuals Made the Difference, Detroit, MI

Background: An investor had a demo lot listed for $38,000. After 43 days with no offers, they added:

- Drone footage
- A modular rendering with yard
- Utility tap confirmation
- Side-by-side before/after graphic

New Offer: $41,500 from a modular home builder within 7 days.

Lesson: The better you tell the story, the faster the right buyer shows up.

Optional Marketing Tools & Enhancers

- Canva Flyer Template (editable)
- QR Code Generator (links to info packet)
- Property Microsite (simple one-page website for the deal)
- Signage + SMS capture ("Text 'LOT123' to 707-888-1234")

- Facebook Lead Ad (hyperlocal targeting)

Use low-cost, high-impact tools to make a $40K lot feel like a $100K opportunity.

Templates to Use

- Lot Listing Template (MLS/Facebook)
- Marketing One-Pager (Lot & Build Versions)
- Email Blast Copy (Builder Outreach)
- Property Info Packet Checklist
- Canva Flyer Templates (Drag & Drop)

Investor Fast-Track Recap

- Package your lot or build like a **product**, not just a property
- Include surveys, zoning docs, visuals, and tap confirmations
- Sell to the right audience: builders, retail buyers, or partner investors
- Use direct outreach, digital folders, and local platforms for reach
- Storytelling + certainty = higher price + faster close

Chapter 13: Case Studies of $0-to-$250K Demolition Deals: Proof That This Works

Quick Start Summary

This chapter brings demolition investing to life through real-world case studies. Each story walks you through how investors identified distressed properties, navigated legal and logistical hurdles, executed demolition, and made calculated exit decisions—resulting in profits from $20,000 to over $200,000.

These deals prove the model works. They also illustrate that success isn't about luck; it's about systems, strategy, and solving overlooked problems. Use these examples as templates and motivation to launch your own profitable demolition journey.

Case Study 01: From Condemned to Cleared Cashout, Kansas City, MO

Deal Type: Boarded-up single-family home with demo order

Purchase Price: $6,000
Demo Cost: $13,200
Site Prep + Survey: $2,800
Total All-In: $22,000

Action Taken:

- Filed FOIA to access city demolition list
- Contacted the owner via skip tracing
- Offered $1,000 and assumed all liens
- Hired demo contractor and completed teardown in 6 days
- Sold the cleared lot to a local builder for $48,000

Timeline: 45 days
Profit: $26,000

Lesson: Speed and simplicity win. When a city wants a nuisance property gone, you create value by removing liability.

Case Study 02: Heir Property Breakthrough, Baltimore, MD

Deal Type: Inherited home with fire damage and tax liens

Title Issues: Deceased owner, no probate filed, 3 heirs in different states
Acquisition Cost: $4,500 + $3,000 to heirs for quitclaim deeds
Demo + Hazmat Clearance: $17,000
Quiet Title Action: $3,800
Total All-In: $28,300

Exit Strategy: Held as a cleared lot with architectural plans

Sold To: Developer building luxury townhomes nearby
Sale Price: $72,500
Timeline: 90 days
Profit: $44,200

Lesson: Solve legal friction others avoid, and you unlock access to major profits. Probate + demolition = control of land.

Case Study 03: $1 Land Bank Acquisition, Cleveland, OH

Deal Type: Demolished lot, city-held

Acquisition Cost: $1
Application Fee + Legal: $750
Builder-Ready Package Design: $2,200 (included renderings + floor plan)
Marketing & Signage: $300
Total All-In: $3,251

Action Taken:

- Submitted redevelopment plan to the city land bank
- Committed to building or flipping within 12 months
- Created flyer package and marketed to 18 local builders
- Sold to builder targeting infill lots for $29,500

Timeline: 28 days
Profit: $26,249

Lesson: When cities give land away, don't question, just prepare. The play isn't the dirt, it's the packaging.

Case Study 04: Build and Flip for Maximum Spread, Indianapolis, IN

Deal Type: Cleared urban lot with ARV upside

Lot + Demo Cost: $18,000
Modular Build (1,350 sf): $141,000
Utilities + Permits: $17,500
Landscaping + Staging: $3,500
Total All-In: $180,000

Exit: Sold for $298,000
Profit: $118,000
Timeline: 6.5 months

Lesson: When comps are strong, and time is on your side, the full build brings the biggest reward. Modular = controlled budget, fixed margin.

Case Study 05: Joint Venture with Builder, Atlanta, GA

Deal Type: Double-lot teardown in a gentrifying corridor

Acquisition Cost: $9,000
Demo: $18,000
Partner Builder: Provided funding + construction
Agreement: 50/50 profit split after costs

Total Project Profit: $204,000
Investor Share: $102,000
Timeline: 7 months
Investor Capital Deployed: $27,000
ROI: ~377%

Lesson: You don't need to build experience to build equity. A great lot, good contractor, and a clean deal structure can turn dirt into a six-figure check.

Summary Table of All Deals

Case	Strategy	All-In	Exit	Profit	Timeline
KC Condemned	Demo + flip lot	$22,000	$48K	$26,000	45 days

Baltimore Heirs	Demo + legal + flip	$28,300	$72.5K	$44,200	90 days
Cleveland Land Bank	Free lot + package	$3,251	$29.5K	$26,249	28 days
Indy Build	Demo + modular build	$180,000	$298K	$118,000	6.5 months
Atlanta JV	Demo + partner build	$27,000	$102K (50%)	$102,000	7 months

What These Deals Have in Common

- They started with problem properties: condemned, inherited, fire-damaged, city-held
- They required paperwork, planning, and patience
- They didn't rely on traditional listings or agents
- They were structured using templates, scripts, and repeatable processes

None of these deals required more than $30K in upfront capital—and most were completed without lending or credit lines.

Investor Fast-Track Recap

- Demolition deals work in every city, but only if you **take the first step**
- Focus on **value creation**: clearing titles, solving legal issues, and prepping lots
- Your profit isn't in drywall; it's in dirt, data, and documentation
- Learn from others, build your system, and take consistent action

Chapter 14: Investor Toolkit & Templates: Systems That Scale and Win

Quick Start Summary

Every successful demolition investor has a system. Not just a gut instinct, but a repeatable, documented, and organized workflow to track leads, assess risk, manage projects, and exit profitably.

In this chapter, you'll receive the core toolkit to run your demolition investing operation like a business. From property evaluation checklists and contractor agreements to lien letters, offer scripts, and builder-ready pitch decks, this toolkit reduces stress, increases efficiency, and lets you scale confidently.

Master these tools, and every new deal becomes a calculated play—not a gamble.

Why Tools Beat Talent

Talent is what you start with. Systems are how you win consistently.

A talented investor can close one good deal. But a *systemized* investor can:

- Track 30+ leads at once
- Follow up with 100+ heirs without confusion
- Submit 5 city proposals per week
- Run simultaneous demo, build, and resale pipelines

Tools = scale, speed, and sanity.

You don't rise to the level of your talent, you fall to the level of your systems.

Core Deal Management Toolkit

Demolition Property Deal Tracker (Google Sheets/Excel)

Columns include:

- Property Address
- Owner Name & Contact
- Source (Demo List / Probate / Fire)
- Status (Contacted, Under Contract, In Court, Closed)

- Title Issues Present?
- Lien Amount
- Estimated Demo Cost
- Exit Strategy
- ROI Projection
- Notes & Follow-Up Date

Use conditional formatting to color-code your hottest leads, overdue tasks, and closed deals.

Property Evaluation Scorecard

Category	Max Points	Sample Notes
Lot Value Potential	10	$65K resale comps nearby
Zoning / Buildability	10	R-3 with duplex allowed
Environmental Issues	10	No asbestos found
Title Status	10	Deceased owner—heirs located
Exit Strategy Fit	10	Modular flip to an FHA buyer
Total Score	**50**	Greenlight if >38

Use this before any offer is made to keep emotion out of the deal.

Legal & Acquisition Documents

Templates Included:

- Quitclaim Deed (Universal Template)
- Demolition Property Purchase Agreement
- Heir Authorization Letter
- Affidavit of Heirship
- City Proposal Cover Letter
- Lien Payoff Request Letter
- Court Petition to Stay Demolition (Editable)

Store a branded version of each document in your cloud folder, ready to send within minutes.

Contractor & Build Templates

What's Inside:

- Demolition Contractor Agreement
- Scope of Work (SOW) Template
- Draw Schedule & Milestone Tracker
- Site Photos Log Sheet
- Final Inspection Request Form
- GC Insurance & License Verification Sheet

These documents keep your build legal, clean, and on schedule, while protecting you from disputes.

Marketing & Exit Tools

Sell Faster With:

- Lot Listing Template (for MLS, Facebook)
- Builder-Ready One-Pager (Flyer/Email)
- QR Code Generator with Link to Info Folder
- Investor Email Blast Copy
- Canva Flyer Template – Editable with Photos/Plans
- Offer Packet Checklist (Survey, Permit, Renderings, Utilities)

Combine into a Google Drive or Dropbox link for buyers, agents, or builders. Keep your link short and branded (bit.ly or Rebrandly).

Team & Scaling Templates

Organize Like an Operation:

- Virtual Assistant Task Board (Trello/Notion)
- Weekly Pipeline Review Template
- City Proposal Tracker (by Department)
- Land Bank Application Template
- JV Agreement with Builder (50/50 Split Template)
- Scale Plan Worksheet (Leads, Team, Revenue Goals)

Know your numbers: how many deals you want, how many offers you must make, and what team members you need to scale.

Where to Store and Access Your Tools

Recommended Setup:

- **Google Drive** for all editable documents
- **Google Sheets** or **Airtable** for deal tracking
- **Trello/ClickUp** for project pipeline
- **Dropbox** or **Notion** for info packets and city forms
- **LastPass or 1Password** for login management

Create a folder system with the following structure:

1. Leads
2. Legal Docs
3. Templates
4. Projects
5. Marketing
6. Exit Reports

Case Study: From Chaos to Control, St. Louis, MO

Without using tools:

- Investor juggling 6 deals with sticky notes and memory
- Missed lien deadlines, lost contact info, and late inspections
- Closed 1 deal in 5 months

With tools:

- Used tracker, timeline sheets, and city proposal templates
- Hired VA to monitor city portals and track heirs
- Closed 4 deals in 60 days, net profit over $91,000

Lesson: Systems don't just save time; they multiply earnings.

Investor Fast-Track Recap

- Build your toolkit once, then use it for every deal
- Track, filter, and follow up with clarity using digital templates
- Brand your documents for credibility and speed
- Use visual dashboards to manage teams, timelines, and tasks
- Treat your business like a professional operation—not a hustle

Chapter 15: Scaling Your Demolition Investment Business: From One Deal to a Full Pipeline

Quick Start Summary

Closing your first demolition deal is a milestone.

Building a repeatable, scalable business that generates six or seven figures per year?

That's the next level.

This chapter shows you how to go from solo operator to organized real estate business by building systems, hiring support, leveraging partnerships, and expanding into new markets.

Whether your goal is five deals per year or fifty, this chapter equips you with the blueprint to scale smart, avoid burnout, and create sustainable, process-driven success.

The Problem with Staying Small

One deal at a time might feel manageable, but it also means:

- You're always starting over
- Your income is inconsistent
- You can't walk away without everything stalling
- You miss out on bigger, multi-deal opportunities

To scale, you need:

- Lead volume (more deals in your pipeline)
- Operational support (VAs, attorneys, contractors)
- Funding relationships (cash, credit, private lenders)
- A documented system (templates, automations, repeatable workflows)

The goal isn't more stress—it's more structure.

Build Your Weekly Operating Rhythm

Weekly Flow:

Day	Action
Monday	Review all leads in pipeline (status + next steps)
Tuesday	Submit FOIA or court requests for new properties
Wednesday	Contact heirs or owners from new list
Thursday	File or follow up on city proposals
Friday	Review deal tracker, team tasks, and new city policies

Use this rhythm to replace randomness with results. When every week builds the next, your business compounds.

Hire Your First Support Roles

You don't need 10 employees to scale; you need **2-3 'right' helpers**.

1. **Virtual Assistant (VA)**

- Scrapes code violations, demolition dockets, probate notices
- Sends outreach emails
- Updates your CRM or tracker
- Manages file organization

Cost: $5-$12/hr (Philippines or U.S.-based)

2. **Real Estate Attorney**

- Files quiet title actions
- Drafts agreements (JV, quitclaims, proposals)
- Interfaces with city/court systems

Retainer or flat fee per service

3. **Demo Contractor & GC**

- Performs fast, clean demolitions
- Provides permit-ready scopes
- Reduces project management time

Build relationships with crews that deliver on time, every time

Automate with Systems and Software

Tool	Purpose
Google Sheets + Zapier	Deal tracker + auto-updates
Trello or ClickUp	Project board for team
Airtable	Lead management with filters
DocuSign + Google Drive	Contract workflow
Bitly or Rebrandly	Branded file links
Calendly	Buyer/partner scheduling

Treat your investment business like a tech startup with real estate as the product.

Expand Into Other Markets

Once you've got a system that works in your city, scale to:

- **Adjacent cities** within the same state
- **Land bank-heavy regions** (e.g., Detroit, Cleveland, St. Louis)
- **Sunbelt boom towns** with infill demand (e.g., Charlotte, Phoenix)

Use data platforms like PropStream or Local Market Monitor to:

- Identify zip codes with low lot costs and rising ARVs
- See where demo budgets are increasing
- Target counties with predictable permitting processes

Raise Capital Strategically

More deals mean more capital.

Sources of Scale Capital:

- Private Money Lenders (friends, doctors, angel investors)
- Hard Money Loans (short-term construction lenders)
- Equity Partners (you do the work, they put up capital)
- Seller Financing (especially on land or low basis lots)
- HELOCs or Business Credit Lines

Build a pitch deck using your case studies and toolkit to raise funds more effectively.

Build Your Demolition Brand

To attract cities, investors, and partners, build visibility.

- Name your company (e.g., "Urban Lot Revival Group")
- Create a basic website (showcase projects + testimonials)
- Add signage to demo lots with contact info
- Post before-and-after photos on Facebook and LinkedIn
- Host a workshop or community cleanup in targeted areas

City staff, land banks, and neighborhood councils will remember you as "the investor who builds after cleaning up blight."

Case Study: Scaling to 10 Deals Per Quarter, Chicago and Gary, IN

Initial Setup:

- 1 VA
- Local title company
- Preferred demo contractor
- Builder partner for modular installs

System:

- Weekly FOIA requests
- Heir contact automation
- City pitch deck submission
- CRM tracking of 80+ leads/month

Results:

- Acquired 23 properties in 9 months
- Cleared, rebuilt, or sold 19
- Total gross profit: $678,000
- Expanded into 2 new counties

Lesson: Scaling isn't about luck—it's about leverage.

Templates for Scaling

- Team Onboarding Manual
- VA Weekly Task Sheet
- Capital Pitch Deck (PPT Template)
- Expansion Market Checklist
- Weekly Operating Scorecard
- Monthly Deal Report Template

Investor Fast Track Recap

- Start small, but systemize early
- Hire help to reclaim your time and reduce mental load
- Use software + templates to remove guesswork
- Expand to new markets with structured outreach
- Build a brand that attracts support from city officials, contractors, and lenders

Chapter 16: Tools, Templates & Case Study Repository (Appendix)

Your Tactical Library for Demolition Investing

This final chapter is your on-demand playbook, housing every document, worksheet, checklist, and case study reference you need to replicate the systems, structures, and deals discussed throughout this book.

This isn't just a reference guide; it's your business-in-a-box. Use it to take action today, train your team, pitch to cities, and execute demolition deals confidently, from $0 lots to $250,000 profit flips.

Index

Tool	Purpose
Demolition Deal Tracker	Monitor lead status, ROI potential, and legal status
Property Evaluation Scorecard	Standardized deal screening (50-point system)
Weekly Pipeline Review Sheet	Accountability tool for scaling
Seller Offer Letter Template	Send offers to absentee owners or heirs
Quitclaim Deed Template	For title transfer on distressed or heir properties
Heir Contact Letter + Script	Outreach to locate and negotiate with heirs
Affidavit of Heirship	Document family relationship when probate isn't filed
City Proposal Template	Submit reuse proposals to land banks or city officials
Petition to Stay Demolition	Legal filing to pause a scheduled teardown

Lien Payoff Request Letter	Request discounted lien release from city departments
Demolition Contractor Agreement	Scope, schedule, and liability coverage agreement
Asbestos Clearance Checklist	Verify compliance with hazmat removal laws
Builder Draw Schedule	Pay contractors based on milestones, not promises
Inspection Log	Track progress and required sign-offs during build
Marketing One-Pager (Canva)	Professional property packet for lot or build resale
Lot Listing Description Generator	Write strong ad copy for listing platforms
Investor Email Blast Copy	Mass send to builders, developers, and cash buyers
Land Bank Application Template	Streamlined submission for discounted lots
JV Profit Split Agreement	Structure partnerships with builders or lenders
Expansion Market Research Sheet	Compare 3 new cities for growth opportunities

Format: All tools are included in Google Docs, Google Sheets, and editable PDF/Word versions.

Case Study Templates

Use these to document and showcase your wins:

- Case Study Snapshot Sheet (1-pager)
- Before / After Photo Grid (for Instagram or city reports)
- Builder Sale Recap (for buyers)
- Modular Home ROI Breakdown Sheet

- Investor Deck Slide (drop-in format for raising capital)

Build your "Track Record Binder" from day one. Every deal is a credential for the next one.

Tool Use Scenarios

When Submitting to a City:

- City Proposal Template
- Contractor Letter of Intent
- Demo Completion Certificate
- Site Plan / Rendering Packet
- Environmental Clearance Report

When Working with Sellers:

- Offer Letter Template
- Quitclaim Deed
- Heir Agreement
- Title Clean-Up Checklist

When Managing a Build:

- GC Scope of Work
- Draw Schedule
- Inspection Log
- CO (Certificate of Occupancy) Checklist

When Selling or Flipping:

- Lot Marketing One-Pager
- Listing Description (Lot vs. Home)
- Flyer Template
- Property Folder Link via QR Code

Printable Worksheets (For Field Use)

- Property Walkthrough Evaluation Sheet
- Demolition Prep Checklist
- Environmental Risk Assessment
- Weekly Lead Follow-Up Log
- Deal Comparison Matrix (Flip vs. Sell Lot vs. JV)

Designed to print and clip to a clipboard during field visits.

Tool Access & Organization System

Recommended Folder Setup:

1. **Leads** → Evaluation scorecards + contact log
2. **Legal** → All contracts, deeds, court filings
3. **Permits & Docs** → Site plans, demo permits, inspections
4. **Marketing** → Flyers, one-pagers, renderings
5. **Sales & Exit** → Final HUD, CO, buyer packets
6. **Templates** → Editable forms & samples
7. **Case Studies** → Track record and summary pages

Store in cloud (Google Drive, Dropbox) and back up to a physical drive monthly.

Bonus Tools You Can Create From These Assets

- Your own **Training Program** for new team members
- A **City Partner Proposal Deck** (PDF or presentation)
- Your **Investor Deal Book** to raise capital or enter new markets
- A "**Builder Bundle**" you sell to other developers (plans + permits)

Investor Fast Track Recap

- The tools are your engine—use them to move faster, smarter, and with confidence
- Stay organized digitally and physically—structure is your scale strategy
- Every deal should leave behind a footprint: a template, a process, and a documented win
- Reuse, improve, and teach these tools as you grow your business

Congratulations! You're Ready.

You now have everything it takes to build a profitable demolition investment business:

- Knowledge
- Structure
- Real-world examples
- Legal & operational systems

- A scalable, repeatable toolkit

All that's left is action.

Condemned doesn't mean worthless.
Forgotten doesn't mean failed.
Buried under rubble lies real estate gold, if you know where to dig.

Go build.

www.ingramcontent.com/pod-product-compliance
Lightning Source LLC
LaVergne TN
LVHW050938210926
848482LV00013B/660
* 9 7 9 8 9 9 9 7 2 8 1 3 5 *